30 Days to a
Stronger Novel

30 Days to a
Stronger Novel

Darcy Pattison

MIMS HOUSE/LITTLE ROCK, AR

Mims House
1309 Broadway
Little Rock, AR 72202
www.mimshouse.com

30 Days to a Stronger Novel / Darcy Pattison

ISBN 978-1-62944-040-8
Ebook ISBN 978-1-62944-039-2
Printed in the United States of America

"I think you must remember that a writer is a simple-minded person to begin with and go on that basis. He's not a great mind, he's not a great thinker, he's not a philosopher, he's a storyteller.
— *Erskine Caldwell*

Table of Contents

A 30-Day Adventure

Welcome to a 30-day adventure in writing and revising your novel. Each day, you'll be challenged with an inspirational quote, a discussion of a small aspect of writing and revising a novel, and a Walk the Talk assignment to put the discussion into practice.

We'll start slow, with a discussion of titles and subtitles, but the discussion soon gets deep and needs some thought. Work steadily through the chapters, just taking one day at a time. Your revision will fail if you just fly through these discussions in a single day. Instead, a successful revision requires you to think, to apply concepts, and the make changes to your manuscript.

If you put in the time, I can't guarantee a perfect novel; but I can guarantee a stronger novel.

Happy writing!

Darcy Pattison

P.S. For the 30 Days to a Stronger Novel online video course, please visit:

MimsHouse.com/courses

1

Watership Down with Armadillos: Titles

What's in a name? That which we call a rose
By any other name would smell as sweet.
*   Romeo and Juliet, Act ii, Sc. 2*
*   William Shakespeare, playwright*

How do you choose a title for your novel? Of course, titles are marketing tools, designed to catch an audience's imagination and get them to pick up the book and look inside.

Titles can and do make a book memorable. Here is a list of possible titles that an author generated for a book: As Others Are; The World's Room, They Who Get Shot; The Carnal Education; An Italian

Chronicle; The Sentimental Education of Frederick Henry. What was the final title? Ernest Hemingway decided on *A Farewell to Arms.*

Another dramatic difference: F. Scott Fitzgerald changed "Hurrah for the Red White and Blue" to *The Great Gatsby.*

Begin with the audience. For a recent book, an animal fantasy about armadillos, I thought carefully about the novel's audience. It's the story of El Garro's clan who travels north, ever northward, driven by a curse that won't let them go home. Who would read the book? What age? What are their interests? What are current favorite books for this demographic?

After researching currently popular books for my target audience, I started making lists. The first list was boring and inappropriate; notice that it is important to create a list without censoring yourself; just turn out ideas. But at some point, you must go back and evaluate the possible titles.

As a way to think of even more titles, I looked up the 100 most famous movie quotes (just Google it) and used it as a jumping off point to create another long list. You could do the same for famous quotes about a subject such as dogs or Cleopatra or China.

I also scanned the story's text, looking for phrases that I could lift out to use. I wanted something metaphoric. An early draft of Carson McCuller's 1940 debut novel was titled, "The Mute," but the published title was *The Heart is a Lonely Hunter*. The metaphor here made it more attractive.

Lists are your friends! Create long lists of titles that tease, shock, titillate, embarrass, or make someone laugh out loud. Hint at what is to come. Your goal is to get a reader to open the book. That's it. After that, your first line takes over the job of keeping them reading.

Finally, I sent the lists to a couple friends and asked for their favorite three titles. Amazingly, I found consensus on one title and went with that one. *Vagabonds* can be described as *Watership Down* with armadillos.

The process of finding a title is sometimes easy, sometimes hard. When it doesn't come easily, I don't leave it up to marketing! I make more lists and get feedback and search for the one title that fits the content best. I know my content better than the marketing people and can make sure the title is appropriate for the material. As a friend advised, live with a title for a couple weeks before you submit or publish, and see if it sticks.

Walk the Talk

Create a list of at least ten possible titles for your novel. Use at least one metaphor. Ask friends to identify their favorite three titles. Decide if you will use the most favorite or stick with your first title.

2

Search Me: Subtitles

A world where everyone creates content gets confusing pretty quickly without a good search engine. – Ethan Zuckerman, media scholar and blogger

For your novel, you should write subtitles that focus on discoverability in electronic search engines.

Subtitles aren't always used for novels, but they have become increasing important because of search engines, whether that's an external search engine like Google or an internal search engine on a site like Wattpad. For non-fiction, authors try to pack the subtitle with every keyword for which a person might search. For fiction, genre words or keywords will help searchers find your book.

Here are two free keyword research tools that don't require you to set up an account. Each will give you slightly different suggestions on keywords for your topic, so you may want use both for the same project.

1. Wordstream Free Keyword Tool: You get 30 free searches at a time. There are lots of ads on the site, but the resulting keywords look good.

http://www.wordstream.com/keywords

2. SEOBook Keyword Tool: This one gives a reasonable keyword list and you can export it as .csv (for a spreadsheet).

http://tools.seobook.com/keyword-tools/seobook/

Another idea is to use genre keywords suggested by Amazon's KDP for Kindle books by genre. See:

https://kdp.amazon.com/help?topicId=A200PDGPEIQX41

Many keywords are expected, but there are some tricky suggestions. For example, if your genre is Children's Fantasy & Magic/Sword & Sorcery, KDP suggests these keywords: sword, sorcery, magic, dragon, quest.

KDP suggests that you use these keywords to tag your books, but why not put them into the subtitle itself?

Subtitles also keep away unwanted attention. For example, I wrote a children's picture book with the title *19 Girls and Me*. It's the story of friendship in a kindergarten class with 19 girls—and one lone boy. Unfortunately, I get many hits from people looking for pornography for 19 girls. If the book had a subtitle, that might have protected it from the wrong sort of search. I wish I had given my picture book this subtitle:

19 Girls and Me: A Tale of Kindergarten Friendship.

That subtitle would have meant that it would be easier for kindergarten teachers to find the book for the beginning of the school year. And it would have kept away the wrong sort of person.

To take advantage of a contemporary retelling of a folk tale, I also added this subtitle to a recent novel: *Saucy and Bubba: A Hansel and Gretel Tale.* With that subtitle, you know exactly what you'll be getting. Take these ideas into account and add a subtitle that will help search engines find your book.

Walk the Talk

Create a list of ten possible subtitles for your novel. Use subtitles that target keywords for search engines, exclude unwanted searches, clarify topics, or set up expectations. Again, ask friends for opinions and decide on the best subtitle.

3
Defeat Interruptions: Chapter Divisions

The initial consideration was that of extent. If any literary work is too long to be read at one sitting, we must be content to dispense with the immensely important effect derivable from unity of impression — for, if two sittings be required, the affairs of the world interfere, and every thing like totality is at once destroyed. -- The Philosophy of Composition, Edgar Allen Poe, poet

What is the best length for novel chapters? How long are your chapters? How long is long enough or too long?

In his book, *Lessons from a Lifetime of Writing: A Novelist Looks at His Craf*t, action/adventure author David Morrell (creator of the Rambo character, among others) says he tries to write short chapters, so that a reader can complete one chapter (or structural unit) at one sitting. He bases his ideas on two essays by Edgar Allen Poe:

1. The Philosophy of Composition
http://www.eapoe.org/works/essays/philcomp.htm

2. The Poetic Principle
http://poe.classicauthors.net/PoeticPrincipleThe/

Part of Poe's discussion is about pacing; it's about keeping the reader's attention. Morrell says he interprets Poe to mean that he should keep his structural units (or chapters) short in order to accommodate the reader's bladder, TV interruptions, phone calls, a neighbor who drops in, etc. Poe's essays are worth reading, as is Morrell's chapter on "The Tactics of Structure."

Of course–a chapter should be as long as it needs to be. But consider shorter chapters that can be read at one sitting.

In my animal fantasy novel, *Vagabonds*, there are 50 chapters for 270 pages, which averages about 5.4 pages/chapter. However, one chapter is eight pages long, while another chapter is only 103 words long.

Walk the Talk

If you have long chapters, find places to divide them into several chapters. Look for places where a cliffhanger could interrupt a scene and create a nice division. Or look for ends of scenes that set up the next scene with some anticipation.

4

Scarlett or Pansy: The Right Character Name

Thrice happy he whose name has been well spelt

In the despatch: I knew a man whose loss

Was printed "Grove," although his name was Grose.

– Don Juan, Canto viii. Stanza 18. Lord Byron, poet and playwright

A rose by any other name might smell as sweet, but do you really want to smell a swamp lily? Doesn't the name "swamp lily" make you want to pinch your nose? Or consider that in early drafts Margaret

Mitchell is supposed to have named her famous heroine Pansy instead of Scarlett O'Hara. Do you believe that Pansy would have done the things that Scarlett did? Never!

Naming characters is important! Here are some things to consider:

1. Can readers pronounce the name? Especially for fantasies and science fiction, beware of invented names that no one can pronounce. Remember how hard and frustrating it is to read all the begets of the *Bible*–and don't do that to your reader.

2. Appropriate for the story? Whether you're writing a contemporary or a story set in the 1030s, use appropriate names for that time period. Try looking at the Social Security Administration's list of popular baby names by year: http://www.ssa.gov/OACT/babyna mes/

3. What does the name mean? Think about the meaning of names. Look for baby name books that explain the meaning behind a name. Often when I'm in the early stages of writing a story, I am more worried about meaning when I want the name to represent something about the character. By the time the final draft is done, I may have forgotten what the name means, but that extra layer of meaning is still there.

My mother tells me, by the way, that the year I was born, the Pet Evaporated Milk Company put out a book of baby names. That's where she found the name, Darcy. (It was years before I ever heard of Mr. Darcy.) Together with my maiden name, my name means Dark Fortress. My husband's name means Blond Warrior. Dark Fortress meets Blond Warrior. Doesn't it sound like a like a marriage made in heaven?

Walk the Talk

Find a book that gives the meaning of names. What do your character's names mean? Does that meaning resonate someway in your story? Consider changing at least one character's name to something more appropriate, more provocative, or just more fun.

5

My Wound is Geography: Stronger Settings

"My wound is geography. It is also my anchorage, my port of call."

— Pat Conroy, The Prince of Tides, novelist

Always try to match the setting to the emotional layers of your story. For example, the setting of *Lizzie Bright and the Buckminster Boy* by Gary D. Schmidt is a New England coastal village, appropriate for several reasons. It's built on a solid cliff, like Turner's life is built on the solid foundation of family and church. Lizzie, the black girl, is physically separated from Turner's life because she lives on an island. And the coast is a place where a boy might row out far enough to come face to face with a whale, a place where a boy might look into the eye of a whale. It speaks of foundations and separations and inspiration and growth.

My particular pet peeve is generic school settings. Yes, to an extent, if you've been in one school, you've been in them all. But teachers—and characterizations of teacher characters are important—can create a microenvironment within a school. Does the teacher in your story have family pictures on his or her desk, or have awards or vacation pictures or just generic posters on the wall?

What is the emotional environment of your story? When you choose a setting, make it echo that emotional environment! This could include the time period, the geographic location, the buildings, the clothing, the time of year, the weather, and the bit characters who populate this setting. Evaluate all these in light of the emotional journey your character is taking.

In the *ALIENS, INC.* series, short chapter books about aliens shipwrecked on Earth, each story begins in art class. In *Kell, the Alien*, Kell makes an Accidental Art. The emotional environment is one of creativity and individuality; certainly aliens are unique. In *Kell and the Horse Apple Parade*, the class is creating art that takes off of Alexander Calder's "Red Nose," which emphasizes differences in alien and human anatomy. *Kell and the Giants* begins with a U.S. map painted onto a tennis court, and of course, our hero paints himself into a corner. The art class is flexible enough to reflect the theme of each book in the series, yet it also gives stability through its repetition.

Does this sound too much like your English class trying to analyze a story? Well, it is.

Another book that provokes me to think about stronger settings is *How to Read Literature Like a Professor: A Lively and*

Entertaining Guide to Reading Between the Lines by Thomas Foster. Here's one tidbit: he asks: when is a meal not just a meal? When it is a communion service among family members, a way to connect them tightly. Look for other intriguing ideas on setting and emotion in Foster's book.

Walk the Talk

Take a look—or take a literal walk— around your setting. Are your characters moving through the setting as the story progresses, or are they always stuck in a cafeteria? What does it mean that the story takes place in this particular geographic spot? Have you used the time of day, the season of the year, or the weather to impact your story? Make three solid changes to your novel's setting.

6

Horse Manure: Stronger Setting Details

*Don't say it was "delightful"; make **us** say "delightful" when we've read the description. You see, all those words (horrifying, wonderful, hideous, exquisite) are only like saying to your readers, "Please will you do my job for me?"*
—C.S. Lewis, novelist and theologian

Where does your story take place? If it's in Barrow, Alaska, then I'd better see the Arctic Ocean, the ice jutting up in sharp columns as it is pushed against the shore. If it's on a horse ranch, when you walk into the barn, I'd better smell horse manure.

You can't just tell a reader that the story is set in the back of a fast food restaurant. The reader should smell stale grease, hear the sizzle of fries cooking, and see the teenage cook with a cold who wipes at his nose with the back of his hand just before he scoops up the fries for the next customer.

If real estate is all about location, location, location, then setting is all about details, details, details. Use every sense: hearing, seeing, tasting, feeling and smelling.

Here's a real-life example: My husband's grandmother was in the hospital, dying from old age: she was 99 years old. The hospital had an infestation of ladybugs, so they were everywhere in her hospital room. Truly, sometimes, life is weirder than fiction. I could have written this:

In the hospital room, ladybugs crawled all over the floor, bed, tables, and light fixtures. It was an odd contrast to the wrinkled old lady who lay dying in the hospital bed.

But the situation could be made more poignant by choosing the right details. This version focuses mostly on visual details, using similes, contrasting descriptions, and other techniques added to the sensory details.

Her thin white hair wisped around her face, making her look like a wrinkled pixie that was lost in the white pillow. Crawling on the pillow, the wall, and in the florescent light above her were hundreds of orange and black ladybugs. They seemed to respect her, staying around her, but never getting on her, as if even their fragile weight would be enough to send her into the next world.

The hospital staff said they had an infestation of lady bugs, which had somehow come in through the ER, and were slowly moving up from floor to floor. As a room became infested, the staff would empty the room and spray–which only managed to send the ladybugs through the ventilation up to the next floor.

When the ladybugs reached the top floor, I asked, would they find their way out and fly up toward the heavens?

Walk the Talk

A good exercise is to write down at least three specific details for each of the five senses before you start writing a scene. By specific I mean as specific as you can make it. Not just a dog. Not just a poodle. But a tawny poodle with unclipped hair that drags its right hind leg when it walks. When you actually write, you may choose to use the more generic description because you don't want to focus that much attention on the dog. But by writing specifics during the prewriting phase, it gives you choices.

Also, as the scene/situation develops and things change, you may need to stop and repeat this so that you are constantly aware of the sensory details. Try to actually use three senses in each scene so that it's anchored in reality.

Tasting and smelling are the hardest senses, depending on the situation, but try hard to write something for these. Please don't fall back on generic descriptions: *it smelled smoky*. That may be fine, but can you sharpen that description by being more specific? *It smelled like burned hair.*

If you have more visual details than anything else, you're probably a visual learner. More auditory details indicate an auditory learner. The point is to learn your bias and then work to strengthen the other senses.

7

Weaklings: Every Character Must Matter

If you're silent for a long time, people just arrive in your mind.
—Alice Walker

Stories are about characters who are involved in a conflict with each other. Often in revising, it's important to look carefully at each character and ask hard questions:

- Does this character contribute to the conflict and resolution?
- What is this character's role in the story? For example, is s/he the protagonist? The mother of the

antagonist? The only butcher? This could be a family role or occupation.

- What is this character's function in the story? Does s/he provide comic relief, deliver bad news, or speak for those who can't speak for themselves?

Often when you evaluate your characters, you realize you have one or more weak characters. What do you do about these weaklings as you revise?

1. Cut. Each character should contribute to the story in some way. Sometimes, characters are just fillers or place holders and don't really contribute. If you totally cut this character from the story, would it substantially change the story? If you answer "no," then cut.

2. Combine. Can you combine this character with another character? By putting more than one function/role into a character, it's possible to create a more interesting character. If you

have two best friends, can you combine them into one?

3. Enrich. If the character's role and function are necessary to the story and you can't combine the character with another, then you must enrich this character. It's back to the drawing board.

In my *Aliens, Inc.* series, the stories about a shipwrecked alien family take place in a school setting, which has the potential for many missteps in adding characters. If Kell's class has 30 students, and the school has a dozen teachers and even more staff, which characters are included in the story? Each book in the series narrows the cast of characters by focusing the plot around one student and one or two teachers.

In *Kell, the Alien*, the focus is on Bree, Kell's neighbor and the music teacher, Mr. Vega. In *Kell and the Horse Apple Parade*, the focus switches to Mary Lee Glendale, the police chief's daughter and the team teachers Mrs. McGreen, the health teacher and Mrs.

Parrot, the science teacher. By focusing each book, I can prevent weak characters.

There's no right or wrong number of characters for a story. What you want are strong characters who can carry their own weight.

Walk the Talk

List your characters, along with the function or role of each one in your story. Look for overlapping roles or functions that will allow you to cut one character or combine two of them. Check for anemic characters who need enrichment, and rethink their characterization from the ground up. If a character doesn't make significant contributions to your story, consider deleting the character.

8

Take Your Character's Pulse

I don't ever write about real people. Art is supposed to be better than that. If you want a slice of life, look out the window.
—Barbara Kingsolver

The emotional arc of a story, the inner conflict, is just as important as the narrative arc, the outer conflict; it's just harder to see sometimes. One way to check this emotional or inner conflict arc is to consider scenes one at a time. (Not sure if you are writing in scenes? Read *The Scene Primer* by Sandra Scofield.) First mark off one scene in your manuscript. Then identify the emotional pulse of the scene, the point at which the emotions come to the surface.

What question needs an answer? Is there an emotion underlying all the action of the scene? Does the character's emotional state differ at the beginning and end of the scene?

For example, this is the second and third paragraph of the opening chapter of *Lizzie Bright and the Buckminster Boy* by Gary D. Schmidt:

"Turner Buckminster had lived in Phippsburg, Maine, for almost six whole hours.

He didn't know how much longer he could stand it."

The emotional stakes are clear: he doesn't want to move to this town.

Often you can identify the exact place where the pulse of a scene quickens. Look for it, and strengthen it. If a scene lacks an emotional center or pulse, find a way to make the emotional arc stronger or to inject new emotions.

In Chapter 3 of my novel, *The Girl, the Gypsy and the Gargoyle*, Laurel watches a Gypsy band as they entertain a crowd with a trained bear who dances with the old Gypsy. In describing the bear, I say:

He looked almost civilized. Except the eyes, which were black and wild.

Laurel is afraid of the wild creature and hopes that the dance will finish without any accident. Fear is the driving force that keeps her watching the performance.

Walk the Talk

Mark off a scene in your novel. What is the emotional heart of this scene? Often, it comes down to a question of relationships: are characters at odds, or getting along? If there is no emotional question in the scene, either add one or omit the scene.

9

Yin-Yang: Connecting Emotional and Narrative Arcs

Find out what your hero or heroine wants, and when he or she wakes up in the morning, just follow him or her all day.
—Ray Bradbury, novelist and short story writer

The emotional arc is the inner conflict; the narrative arc is the outer conflict. Like dark and light, or yin-yang, the two must mesh seamlessly.

Peter Dunne, in his book *Emotional Structure: Creating the Story Beneath the Plot* has a simple suggestion. Dunne says to write a headline summarizing the plot points of a scene on an index card, and jot a few notes about the action, being careful to only hit high points. Turn the card over and write a headline for the emotional content of this scene and jot a few notes about how the emotions change, being careful to only hit high points. I've been using a spreadsheet to keep track of my scenes, so I just added a column for emotion.

Here's how it looks for the first three chapters of my fantasy novel, *The Girl, the Gypsy and the Gargoyle.*

1. Headline: Wherein the Girl, the Gypsy and a Gargoyle run into each other.

Action: Laurel helps her father check the Cathedral of St. Stephen's statues for winter damage and when one heavy statue falls toward Father, a Gypsy boy shoves him out of the way, saving his life.

Emotion: Laurel longs to be a stone sculptor. Fear her father will be hurt.

Surprise and interest in the gypsy boy who seems to appreciate the cathedral's beauty.

2. Headline: Wherein a priest is shown to have a heart of stone.

Action: Laurel shows Father's blueprint for the West Towers to Father Goosens (Goosawn), who says there is no money to add a new tower to the cathedral.

Emotion: Pride in father's design. Surprise and disappointment in Father Goosens's decision. Determination to change his mind.

3. Headline: The old Gypsy and the bear and the dance of death.

Action: Gypsies perform to earn money and Laurel is drawn to watch. However a street gang interrupts the dance, provoking the bear to injure the old Gypsy.

Emotion: Fear. Anger. Anxious to help.

Turning the card over (or filling in an extra column) forces me to consider what my character would really feel in this situation. And it connects the inner and outer conflict in a simple, yet powerful way. After I know the right emotions, it's easy to integrate them into the story.

Walk the Talk

Buy a pack of index cards. For each scene, take an index card and jot down the scene's headline or summary, and then add action on one side and the scene's emotion on the other side. Work to tailor the scene's action and emotions until the inner and outer arc are intertwined.

10

Owls and Foreigners: Unique Character Dialogue

The poor novelist constructs his characters; he controls them and makes them speak. The true novelist listens to them and watches them function; he eavesdrops on them even before he knows them.
—André Gide, novelist

When characters speak, their dialogue should be distinctive. Yet, when I write, if I'm not careful, I tend to have all characters talk like–well, talk like me. Not good. Here are two ideas to try.

1. Separate files. One revision strategy that seems to help is to cut and paste a character's dialogue into a separate file. Then read straight through that file and listen carefully for consistency, uniqueness, etc. Or compare two characters' dialogue files and see if they are too similar.

2. Study dialects. Another good idea is to study regional differences and the sounds of foreign languages. When I'm looking for a unique voice, I study dialects from various parts of the U.S. Often, dialect descriptions get lost in the way sounds are made; this would only result in funny spellings for words. Instead, I'm looking for syntactic differences, or how sentences are structured.

An example would be the use of the negative-positive in Bostonian English: "Let's go see if we can't get your car fixed." Of course, you can emphasize the accent with the extra strange spelling: "Yoah cah." But I think the sentence structure goes a long way toward making the voice distinctive without the difficulties of special spelling. The goal is unique characters, not hard-to-read dialect.

In my animal fantasy, *Vagabonds*, the barn owl Blaze talks in a unique manner. Her speech is clipped short, with simple sentence structures.

> *Blaze snapped her beak. Her talons gripped the tree limb tighter, knocking off bits of bark. "Don't know. Huge nest. Built on old nests. That's what the barn owl said. You look, you decide."*

Walk the Talk

Cut and paste one character's dialogue into a separate file, using just the words they actually say and no actions or "s/he said" phrases. Repeat for other characters. Evaluate the dialogues separately. Does the character stay in character or are there times s/he sounds like someone else?

Enlist a couple friends to help, and ask each friend to choose one character to read aloud for you. As they read, watch for places where they stumble over words because the dialogue isn't right for that character. If no friends are available, use a text-to-speech program (such as what comes pre-installed on iOS Mac computers: System Preferences / Dictation and Speech) to listen to each character's dialogue using a different voice. Make any changes you feel necessary.

11

Sneaky Shoes: Inner and Outer Character Qualities

These characters in my mind are not real. They aren't. When a character puts me under house arrest, I have to remember that I can escape.
—Michael Cadnum, poet and novelist

Sol Stein's book, *Stein on Writing*, has one of the best tutorials on character descriptions. Stein–like every other fiction writing teacher–mentions five ways to characterize: physical attributes, clothing, psychological mannerisms, actions, and dialogue. But consider this description from his book:

"She always stood sideways so people could see how thin she was."

This line does double duty, letting the reader know something about the internal characteristics of the character (the attitudes of the character) at the same time we learn how skinny she is.

Here's another from Stein:

"She bombarded them with questions nonstop as if their answers were irrelevant."

I find this line less effective. We do know internal characteristics: the woman is self-centered and arrogant. However, I think it would have been more effective if some physical dimension of her voice had been included, too. I might have added:

With a cigarette-hoarse voice, *she bombarded them with questions nonstop as if their answers were irrelevant.*

Try to make your character descriptions do the double duty of characterizing both internal and external characteristics in an economy of words.

In *Kell and the Horse Apple Parade, Book 2, The Aliens, Inc.* series, the school Principal, Mrs. Lynx is president of the Society of Alien Chasers. Of course, Kell must be very careful around her so she doesn't figure out he's an alien. Here's how she is first introduced in this story:

"But just then, Principal Lynx came into the room. She wore barefoot shoes, the kind that shows each toe. They were sneaky shoes."

Just by a description of her shoes, the reader understands that Principal Lynx is playing detective and trying to unmask aliens.

Walk the Talk

For your main character, write down two characteristics, one inner and one outer. Write a one-line description that combines both.

12

Friends or Enemies: Consistent Character Relationships

"A human being is nothing but a story with skin around it."
—Fred Allen, humorist

In my novel, *The Girl, the Gypsy and the Gargyole*, I worked hard to keep character relationships are consistent. Laurel, the main character has three main relationships in the story: with Jassy, her Gypsy friend and traveling companion, with her father and with the villain, the Gargoyle Man.

Among other things, a first reader pointed out some inconsistencies in these relationships. This was an important enough observation to spend some focused time revising. First, I re-read the manuscript and found the places where the main character interacts with each of the others.

It was actually fairly easy because each interaction had about three chapters. I physically separated these into three stacks of paper and then marked them up. I was looking for emotional content, reactions to each other, all those small things that create a relationship. Surprisingly, these interactions take only a small space in a chapter/scene. You've got to keep the action going along, and the plot takes up a lot of space. There's description and dialogue. There's emotional stuff in all of this because you can and should color any of it with an attitude. But surprisingly little directly reflects the relationship between two characters.

Next, I needed to decide on what the relationship should be—actually the hardest task of all. For a father-daughter relationship, should the father be wishing for a son, instead of a daughter? Or does he support his daughter in all her hopes and dreams? Of course, we know what the perfect father would do. But this is fiction: it's about dysfunctional families and the ways in which relationships can get tangled up. Once I decided that the father really wanted a son, it meant revising the small exchanges that revealed this. After that, I repeated the process for the other two relationships. Jassy is always a friend. The relationship with the villain is always a conflict between enemies.

It's easy to gain consistency in relationships by looking at this issue separately from plot, dialogue or setting. Focusing a revision on one problem at a time is a good revision strategy.

Walk the Talk

Using a specific color highlighter or pen, mark up text that indicates the relationship between two characters. Read over the highlighted areas to see if you portray the relationship in consistent language. Make any changes necessary. Repeat with a different color for a different relationship.

13

Set Up the Ending: Begin at the Beginning

Cross out every sentence until you come to one you cannot do without. That is your beginning.
—Gary Provost, writing teacher

Where to begin your novel? That is the question. When you write the first draft, you should just jump in and get started. But when you revise your novel, you have a better chance of making the right choice by choosing the best revision strategy.

1. Connect the beginning and the end. Make sure the beginning sets up the ending.

If you solve the problem of a character wanting to make new friends, then the ending needs to reflect the resolution of that problem. If the beginning and end don't match up, you can decide if you want to change the ending or the beginning but they must match up.

2. Set the tone. Make sure the tone–the attitude displayed by the choice of vocabulary, sentence structure, genre, etc.– sets up the rest of the story.

3. Consider beginning much later (or much earlier). Often, it takes writers a while to get started in a story. Open your manuscript to page 25. Consider starting your story near here. Would you really miss anything from the first 25 pages? Open to page 50. Would this be an even better place to start?

On the other, I always have to expand my stories, which means I usually need to start earlier and include a chapter of introduction of the characters and what is at stake.

In *Book 1, The Aliens Inc.* series, *Kell, the Alien,* I had to decide where to start not just a single book, but also a whole series. I left out the backstory of how the aliens shipwrecked and focused on how the aliens would earn a living. Everything starts in an elementary school classroom with a discussion between Bree and Kell. Bree says she wants an alien-themed birthday party, and when Kell realizes Bree's mom will pay for party planning, he volunteers his family. It sets up the themes of Book 1 and the rest of the series.

Walk the Talk

Look over your last few stories to see if there's a pattern: do you tend to start too early or too late? Knowing your biases can help you figure out the best opening.

If you start too early, look at page 25 and page 50. Would either of those be a better place to start?

If you start too late, introduce the characters better and establish the story's stakes right away.

14

Bang, Bang! Ouch! Scene Cuts

When plot flags, bring in a man with a gun.
—*Raymond Chandler, novelist*

Readers today like fast-paced novels. Yet, too fast a pace confuses the reader. When you revise your novel, you can solve this imbalance by paying attention to transitions.

The most important thing to establish in a transition from one scene to the next is to re-orient the reader to the time and place the action is occurring. Where are we? TV and movies do this easily with the visual details. In writing, we often need to put in indications of time (three hours later), setting (Later, in the living room), relationship to plot elements (after the argument), and emotion (Weeping at the loss of her dog).

I especially find that chapter beginnings need better orientation. For the writer, one scene follows logically from the previous. Since chapter breaks are good stopping points, the reader may have put the book down, gone to school, studied for a test, or attended a football game before finally getting back to your story. Make sure they are re-oriented at each chapter opening.

Here are some chapter openings from my book, *Aliens, Inc.* series, *Book 3, Kell and the Giants*. Notice that each opening has a phrase that re-orients the reader:

Chapter 2: At home, Bree and I made peanut butter sandwiches. . .

Chapter 3: On Mr. Martinez's desk stood something tall. . .

Chapter 4: All that week, Mrs. Lynx and Gloria patrolled the hallways. . .

Chapter 5: I had decided to make five maps.

Chapter 6: Bang, bang! Ouch! Dad hit his thumb with a hammer.

Chapter 7: Dark clouds filled the sky on Geography Day.

Chapter 8: The day of the Giant party, it rained.

Chapter 9: The Giant party started late.

Chapter 10: No! I couldn't let the S.A.C win. I pushed through the crowd. . .

TV and movies practice rapid scene cuts. One suggestion is to watch the TV drama "CSI" for great scene cuts. Often, a detective will find a clue that could have important ramifications, depending on how the lab results turn out. Instead of tediously showing the lab work taking place each time, the writers make the assumption that the reader will understand that the lab work did indeed occur. So, the next scene shows the detective questioning the suspect. Notice, they also skipped the scenes where they obtained an arrest warrant and actually went out to pick up the suspect. Those actions are unimportant to the CSI plot.

Sometimes the transition between scenes is a perfect place for characters to take time and give their emotional reaction to the story events. Emotional reactions can be while they are alone, or they can include dialogue with someone else. The emotional section can be short: *Angrily, he left the room and. . . (next scene).* Or, it can take several pages in which a character considers many options for action. Keep the tension as high as possible, and if the reflection is long, follow with an action-packed scene. Either way, the reflection should lead to a new decision about what to do next, which leads into a new scene and new action.

Walk the Talk

In your story look for places where you can leave out tedious details and safely assume the audience will understand what happened between scenes. Watch and study scene cuts in CSI episodes and your favorite action-adventure movies. Also, check your chapter opening to be sure the reader is re-oriented and knows when and where the story is resuming.

15

Go Away! Take a Break

To be happy, you must have something fulfilling in your life that has nothing to do with your work, because there's a terrible tendency to wait for the phone to ring. I want my life to feed the work. I don't want it to be something that happens only between jobs.

—Barbara Hershey, actor

One of the most important things I do to improve my novel is to take a break. Sometimes, I'll indulge in my favorite hobby, quilting. I may attend a quilting workshop or just do a day of marathon sewing, playing with color instead of with words. Or, I may go on a long bike ride and picnic.

Whatever your hobby, a one-day break is often enough to refresh and bring you back ready to work. It's only a one-day break, though. Come back tomorrow ready to work!

Let me just say it: You have permission to take a one-day break.

Walk the Talk

Go! Do something fun. Be with friends and family for a day off.

You may also find value in taking a longer break from your story after finishing a full draft or full revision. Put your current work-in-progress in a drawer and refuse to read it for a month. Or three months. You'll come back to it fresh and ready to work.

16

Power Abs for Novels

The only authentic ending is: John and Mary die. John and Mary die. John and Mary die. *So much for endings. Beginnings are always more fun. True connoisseurs, however, are known to favor the stretch in between, since it's the hardest to do anything with.*

—*Margaret Atwood, novelist and poet*

One of the hardest tasks to accomplish with a plot is to keep the middle from sagging. The opening is full of action, and the ending brings all the plot elements together into a big scene. But that middle! What to do about it?

Peter Dunne proposes an unusual paradigm for the middle of a story in his book, *Emotional Structure: Creating the*

Story Beneath the Plot. Although it was written for screenwriters, the principles still hold for novelists. Dunne says that the beginning and ending are about plot, or the outer problem. The middle is about what he calls "story," what most of us would call the inner problem. Beginning (Act 1) and ending (Act 3) both focus on action. The middle (Act 2) is all character.

Or, Dunne says, you can do just the opposite. The beginning and ending focus on character, while the middle is all action. Instead of integrating the outer and inner, this strategy suggests that you focus on one or the other in Act 2, leaving the opposing arc for Acts 1 and 3.

In my novel *Saucy and Bubba: A Hansel and Gretel* tale, Acts 1 and 3 focus on Saucy's relationship with her father and stepmother. Act 2 finds Saucy trying to survive on her own while taking care of her younger brother. Character, action, character. It's a structure that adds clarity to Saucy's story.

Walk the Talk

In your story, do you integrate the inner and outer story arcs, or do you focus on one for certain parts of the story? When you're plotting with this strategy, it means that you need to think of the character's inner arc, their growth, what makes them change, and how do they change. Write out six or more steps of that emotional growth and specifically, what provokes each step. Then, go back to the outer arc, the plot, and slot in events. Do they progress in parallel steps, or does one come to the forefront for Act 2? Whichever strategy you choose, work to sharpen the inner and outer arc and how they affect each other.

17

White Rocks Lead Me Home: Epiphanies

I experienced writer enlightenment as I was writing kids' mid-year progress reports. I realized that I couldn't write one more "Jennifer needs to take more risks to become a better learner" until I did what I was asking them to do. I took off the next year of teaching to write.

—Jon Scieszka, picture book writer

An epiphany is a strong moment in the character's narrative arc in which they learn something or realize something. If a climax scene is the highest moment of the plot, an epiphany is the highest moment of the character arc.

Unfortunately, there are many ways for epiphanies to go wrong.

"As the light faded, Abigail smiled at the words from the angel. Suddenly, she realized that she needed to forgive that ruffian Juan for his cruelty."

Clichés and flowery language do not work for an epiphany. An angel rarely appears to deliver the lesson with golden lights and resonant words.

Instead, plan ahead for an epiphany. Set up the changes that a character needs to make in order to take the next step in the story. Make sure your inner character arc leads realistically to a character's epiphany.

Consider using symbolism, or allowing some object in the story to take on a deeper meaning. In my novel, *Saucy and Bubba: A Hansel and Gretel Tale,* I use the folktale's trail of white rock to give hope that someday Saucy will find her way home again.

Use action to indicate a heart-felt change. In Elaine Marie Alphin's novel, *Perfect Shot*, her main character realizes that team work and trust is important; it's at that point that he passes up a shot and gives the ball to a better shooter, one who wins the game for them.

Look for other ways to deliver an epiphany–without the angel!

Walk the Talk

First, identify an epiphany. What does your character learn or realize in the course of the story? What character changes take place because the character is in this set of circumstances?

Next, find the place where you express that change. Often it works to include a before and after look at the character. This can be long and involved such as Scrooge's transformation in Dicken's *A Christmas Carol*. In the beginning, Scrooge is miserly to the poor, to his nephew and to the Cratchit family. Later, he is generous to exactly the same people. But it can also be short, just a phrase at the beginning that is echoed with important changes at the end.

Look for objects in the story that could take on some sort of symbolism. Here's an example from my days as a Freshman Composition teacher: one essay focused on the story of a girl's high school basketball career. It ended with the girl coming out of the locker room after the last game of her senior year. Her father saw her come out and tossed her a basketball. She cupped the ball and realized that for four years, basketball had been her world, and she was leaving it behind. The shape of the basketball—like a globe—lent itself to the symbolism of a world filled with basketball. And a humble object took on added importance. Look for and treasure objects when they have the power to carry the emotional weight of an epiphany.

18

The Final Showdown

I always wanted to write a book that ended with the word mayonnaise.
—*Richard Brautigan, novelist*

You've written a wonderful novel. The reader has stayed up late to finish it and they turn the page for the climax scene and read, *"The next morning, after it was all over, Jeremiah mulled over his feelings."*

What? You didn't write the climax?

It happens. A writer gets to the climax, to the scene of great emotional power and somehow the emotions that s/he must face to write that scene seem too overpowering. The writer skips the scene and goes directly to the aftermath.

No! Write the climax!

Some tips for revising the climax of your novel:

1. Consider setting. What settings have the most emotional power in your story? Can you set the climax there? One common element is to put the climax in a high place, like a bridge, top of a skyscraper, etc., symbolizing that this is the high point of the story and the scene with the most emotional danger. Is there a place like that anywhere in your story's world?

2. Consider length. The climax should be the most emotionally powerful scene, and partly that means it should be one of the longest scenes in the novel. It should be extended with twists, surprises, or the mini-climaxes of sub-plots. Length doesn't necessarily equal emotional power, but done right, it can add to the suspense, tension, and emotions.

3. Consider the final confrontation. The climax should be the final

confrontation between the antagonist and protagonist. Seems obvious, but it's so easy to slip up and make it between that protagonist and another minor character.

4. Consider the romantic subplot. If you have a romantic subplot, it is the only subplot that is typically resolved after the main conflict. After all the problems are taken care of, then the lucky couple can get together.

The reader has stayed up for hours while you finished your tale. Don't disappoint them.

In my story, *Saucy and Bubba: A Hansel and Gretel Tale*, Saucy and Daddy have a showdown, of course. For me, it's always been puzzling that the folktale didn't include a confrontation between child and father. He merely accepts them when they return home. In my story, I extend the confrontation scene over a couple chapters and fully explore the idea of a blended family and the difficulties inherent in it.

Walk the Talk

Answer these questions about the climax of your story. After answering, rewrite the climax as needed:

- Did you write the climax?
- Are the antagonist and protagonist present?
- Are the antagonist and protagonist in direct conflict?
- How many pages does it take up? Can you extend the scene with surprises, twists, reversals or other techniques?
- Is the climax full of emotional upheaval?
- Does the climax resolve the story question set up in the story's opening?

19

One Year Later: Tie up Loose Ends

An author ought to write for the youth of his own generation, the critic of the next, and the schoolmaster of ever afterwards.
—*F. Scott Fitzgerald, novelist*

I just finished reading a fantasy novel that left half of the subplots hanging. Yes, yes, I know. They are setting up for a second book. But it's aggravating for readers.

Look over your novel once more. Are there any subplots left unresolved? Are there any questions about the characters that you brought up, but didn't answer?

Don't think you have to totally solve everything. Sometimes a change comes in the character's attitude, and while the situation remains unresolved, the reader understands that the new attitude will carry the character through the coming days.

My novel, *Vagabonds*, an American fantasy about armadillos in the Ozark Mountains, ends with a chapter entitled, "One Year Later." It's a brief chapter, which shows Galen, the main character, with his family a year later and demonstrates how the fate of armadillos has changed. It's a short, two-page wrap up that is effective and economical.

Walk the Talk

Play fair. Answer questions you set up, but don't be afraid to leave difficult situations for the protagonist to face with renewed hope. Stories need a sense of closure, even if you don't resolve everything.

Decide what issues need resolution and what you can leave unresolved in your story. But err on the side of resolution so you don't aggravate your readers.

20

Great Deeds: Find Your Theme

A novel is a question, not an answer.
—Richard Peck, novelist

The take-away, or the theme of a story, seems like a mysterious thing sometimes. I usually don't worry much about this in the first draft of a novel, but it's good to consciously address it in revision.

Unfortunately, the problem with theme is that it can be stated in various ways. In my American fantasy novel about armadillos, *Vagabonds,* here are some ways you might state the theme:

- P. 63 Great deeds are often accomplished by normal folk who refuse to give up.

- P. 87 If things were different, your father and I could make our home here. . .Instead, we search for a future and a hope.
- P. 266 What was meant as a curse, was really a blessing.
- P. 263 He had been foolish not to ask for help until it was too late. He needed his Four Sisters, all the Diego family, all of his people. He needed help, and Corrie was freely offering it.

Just trying to clearly and effectively state the theme for yourself is hard! Further complicating things, the external and internal arcs can each have their own respective themes. For the character arc, what is s/he struggling to understand? How does s/he change over the course of the story? If you took a scene from the beginning and one from the end, what differences define the character at the end?

For the external arc, what is the story goal? Try to state it clearly as in the example, "Great deeds are often accomplished by normal folk who refuse to give up."

Once you clearly state the theme, there are several things to look at, and we'll talk about that in tomorrow's discussion.

Walk the Talk

Look at a character's internal arc and determine the theme, or the big ideas that it talks about. Repeat this for the action or external plot. For advanced credit, repeat for any subplots. You may find the theme expressed in slightly conflicting ways. Work to make sure there is consistency across your novel.

21

The Wide, Bright Lands: Theme Affects Setting

Setting details are multipurpose, multitasking tools, and have been described as a literary Leatherman. When a reader first opens a story, setting is the doorway through which he or she ventures into the story events.

—Jessica Page Morrell, editor and writing teacher

Let's assume this is the theme for my novel: We are searching for a place that will give us a future and a hope.

Given that theme, I'll need to think about settings in which my characters live. Are they forced to move on? Why? How? What sort of place would offer them the home they seek? How will they know when they find it?

In the climax scene of *Vagabonds*, my armadillo fantasy, Galen realizes that their great trek across the "wide, bright lands" has brought them greatness as a people:

> *"Galen thought about the trek of his people from the jungles in the far, far south, through the plains of the south, over mountains, through more jungles, across the arid lands of northern Mexico and Texas, to these green valleys of the Ozarks. In all those places were the dens of his people. The trek had made of them a great nation."*

Here, I found the emotional landscape of the story, the setting that underlies the theme.

Walk the Talk

Look in your story to find ways to strengthen the theme through setting. You might find it in:

- The historical time period you choose for the story: a story about loneliness could have power if set in the pioneer prairies.
- The weather: A windy coastline might be a setting for a story about restlessness.
- The clothing: Stuffy Victorian clothing with high collars, long sleeves, and long skirts tells of a repressed spirit.
- The food: For a kid who feels smothered by his parents, feed him liver smothered in onions.

Your theme should be echoed in many of the choices you make about setting.

22

Raccoons, Owls, and Billy Goats: Theme Affects Characters

The wastepaper basket is the writer's best friend.
—Isaac Bashevis Singer, novelist

If the theme dictates much of the setting of a story, it also affects the characters and actions of a story.

Remember the theme of *Vagabonds*, my armadillo fantasy: We are searching for a place that will give us a future and a hope.

What actions are implied by that theme? Traveling in search of a home. Some will protest the travel and search, and some will embrace it.

That was easy. What else?

Well, we know from the setting that they will travel through the Ozark Mountains.

Anything else? Yes. They will encounter Ozark creatures along the way. I planned for those encounters by creating animal characters that could help or hinder their search. Gillett, the old and wise raccoon, gives them advice. Screech owls bring news from home. Billy goats block the easiest paths.

Walk the Talk

List the places where your theme and the story's characters collide. Ask, what else does the theme demand from the characters?

Work to deepen the conflicts, polarize the positions of competing points of view, and connect these with your theme. Don't try to be subtle here; make the connections crystal clear so the theme is obvious to the reader.

23

Side Trips: Choosing Subplots

Another danger is stories that veer off in too many directions because writers tack on subplots or introduce new characters. This danger can be averted by making certain that additions are clearly linked to the ending and by typing up some of the subplots before the climax.

—Jessica Page Morrell, editor and writing teacher

Because novels are a long form of storytelling, they provide the author with space to comment on a theme from multiple perspectives, including side trips here and there. In other words, novels include subplots. You might take a side trip to act as a tour guide in a foreign land (such as the middle school across town!), to give extensive backstory, or even to give comic relief. The subplot, though, is more than just side trips. Instead, it's a set of cohesive actions with its own main characters, goals, setbacks and resolutions.

There are two main types of subplots:

- Main character's secondary concerns and goals. The main character can have more than one goal, usually relating to the main goal in some way. Romantic subplots are a common type.

- Secondary character's concern and goal. One of the other characters is the hero of his/her own plot.

The key for all subplots is that they relate to the main plot and intersect with it in some way. In my chapter book, *Aliens, Inc.* series, *Book 1, Kell, the Alien*, the main plot is about Kell's family figuring out how to earn a living on Earth. One subplot revolves around who will get to sing a solo for a school concert.

Another subplot is the friendship between Bree and Kell. One side trip is Kell's ongoing fear of Earthling bugs, which makes for a series of running gags.

The school concert lets me comment on a side issue of how kids get along in school. The ongoing friendship issue reveals contrasting points of views, and it serves to raise stakes in the main plot. Other uses of a subplot include deepening characterization through variety or contrast, providing plot twists, etc.

To develop a subplot, repeat the same steps as for the main plot, except that the subplot will be simpler, with fewer steps between the conflict and resolution.

Subplots can be introduced and resolved in just a couple chapters. For example, a chase scene that extends over three chapters in the middle of the novel could be a red herring, but gives tension for that sagging middle.

Subplots can also be introduced in the first or second chapter and have threads throughout until the end. The common practice is to resolve all subplots before the main plot, with the exception of the romance subplot, which by convention is resolved last.

In *Kell, the Alien*, Bree makes a startling discovery in the last chapter that will forever change their friendship.

Don't let subplots be haphazard or under-developed. Give them the same thought and care you give the main plot. Just keep them in scale to the main plot.

Walk the Talk

Identify your story's subplots. Now, plot the subplot. That is, decide on the theme, the opening, the middle, and the end. Develop the subplot by adding some plot points in the middle. Make sure the subplot's ending ties into the main plot in important ways.

24

Of Parties, Solos, and Friendships: Knitting Subplots Together

Inspiration usually comes during work, rather than before it.
—Madeline L'Engle, novelist

Let's say you have three subplots. How do you keep them straight and all relevant to the main plot? You knit them together!

It's a good idea to take time to build in connections. These subplots don't take place in isolation, but in the context of the overall story. Look for ways to tie them together.

In my chapter book, *Aliens, Inc.* series, *Book 1, Kell, the Alien,* the main plot of aliens making a living on Earth is tied to the friendship plot because Bree is looking for a party planner, and Kell sees that as an opportunity for his family to start a business. But their relationship develops apart from the party planning business as they interact in the other subplot of the school concert. They both compete to be the soloist, and Kell is miffed when Bree wins. The resolution of the concert ties into the party planning business by suggesting a solution to the problem of two parties scheduled at the same time. The tight interweaving of plot and subplot is exactly what you should strive for.

Walk the Talk

List the main characters, settings, emotions, and events of each plot (used here to mean plot or subplot) using a large sheet of paper and one column for each plot. Then look for ways you can connect the plots.

Each main character is probably involved in at least two plots, maybe more. Can you reuse settings across plot lines? Can an event in the main plot have ramifications for the subplots? Are similar emotions displayed across plot lines? How can something in a subplot raise the stakes in the main plot? Build in as many connections as possible!

Then look at a list of scenes for the various plots, and try to arrange them in the most dramatic way. Maybe one plot gets to a high point and you leave the reader hanging in suspense while you cut to developments in another plot. Maybe you need a scene from this plot to raise the stakes in the other plot. Think hard about the suspense and tension created by the sequencing of scenes.

25

Feedback: Types of Critiquers

Stop! Really stop when someone is complimenting you. Even if it's painful and you are not used to it, just keep breathing, listen, and let yourself take it in. Feel how good it is. Build up a tolerance for positive, honest support.

—Natalie Goldberg, poet and writing teacher

You need feedback on your novel. That's a given. Be careful who you ask for feedback. There are a variety of critiquing styles.

1. Grammar Witch: This person always finds the punctuation, spelling, and grammar mistakes; I'm grateful for them, because fixing what they notice is easy.

2. Line Editor: This person rewrites lines by omitting words, moving things around, or just rewriting a sentence here or there. I appreciate the efforts of this person, but I don't always do what they suggest. I consider everything they suggest, but I also take into consideration the voice of the piece, and sometimes what the Line Editor has done is put the sentence into their voice, destroying the rhythms of my voice. Sometimes their suggestion to omit a word is right on. Or they've noticed that I've repeated, "whirl," ten times in this chapter and they are right that I should drag out a thesaurus. Overall, my attitude towards them is one of caution.

3. Big Picture Critiquer: The hardest critiquers to find are those who can look at the shape of the overall story and see where there are holes in the story logic, where the pacing is off, where the characters are flat, where dialogue is boring, etc. But, for me, these are the most valued critiquers. This is why I always want my critiquers to read the

entire story at one time, even if it's a rather long novel.

Sometimes, this type of critiquer is the quietest in the bunch and you have to listen carefully. For example, once a group went over my work-in-progress with enthusiasm, but as I was leaving, one person said casually as we were walking out the door, "Really, though, I don't think you'll get it published until you resolve the parent-child relationship."

Whoa! That was a great Big Picture Comment, but it was made casually, almost apologetically. Fortunately, I realized the importance of that comment—the most valuable comment of the hour's critique.

4. Under-Confident Critiquer: This person looks at a published writer and says to themselves, "Oh, gee, I can't say anything to them because they are published and they know everything." Sorry, but publication of one book doesn't mean you write the next one perfectly. Even writers with 100 books out need honest feedback from honest

readers. I avoid these critiquers because they aren't helpful.

Walk the Talk

What kind of critiquer are you? Different types of critiquers are needed at different times in a novel's development: don't be shy to claim the title of Grammar Witch, Line Editor, or Big Picture Critiquer. If you're an Under-Confident Critiquer, however, work to make your voice heard.

What kind of critiquers are your friends and critique partners? Again, there's no right or wrong sort to associate with. However, if you only have a Grammar Witch around, you'll want to look for more variety in your feedback partners.

26

Feedback: What You Need from Readers

People want to know why I do this, why I write such gross stuff. I like to tell them I have the heart of a small boy—and I keep it in a jar on my desk.
—Stephen King

Besides a good critique group or an editor you can "trust with a draft," you can also use "naive" readers, or those who know nothing about the writing process.

For these readers, you have some simple instructions.

1. Read the story and enjoy it. But pay attention to how you are *feeling* as you read.

2. When you come to a place that is confusing to you, write a big C in the margin.

3. When you come to a place that is boring, write a big B in the margin.

4. When you come to something that you don't believe would happen in this story, put a big D in the margin.

That's it. You don't want their ideas on how to make it better. You don't want them to mark misspelled words or punctuation. Oh, OK, if they are obsessive, and it makes them feel better—no, even then, that's not their job. Their only job is to pay attention to their feelings as they read.

Now, you can't argue with their opinion. Nor can you ignore their opinion. It's simply how they felt as they read and you must consider if other readers will feel the same.

Another option for feedback is reading aloud to an audience. Here's a report on doing that with six-grade students:

http://www.darcypattison.com/voice/audie
nce-considerations/

Critique group, trusted editor, "naive" readers, or reading aloud to kids–each method of getting feedback has pros and cons. The important thing is to get feedback of some kind. Writing is communication and you must check how it is understood or misunderstood.

Walk the Talk

Decide how you will get feedback on your stories. Write directions to your beta (draft) readers, using the three points listed above. Now, take a deep breath and send your story to the readers. Take courage: they are on your side, and their feedback will only make the story stronger.

27

Stay the Course

This is not a novel to be tossed aside lightly. It should be thrown with great force.
—Dorothy Parker, humorist

Revision can often be a long, drawn-out affair. Work, school assignments, family, illness, life crises–many things can interrupt the novel revision process. Expect it.

Of those reading this now, beware. Some of you will have a car wreck in the next month or so. Some will have a major computer crash. Some will experience illness. Some will experience loss of a family member. Some will get married! Grief, love, despair, joy, vacations, trips, births, deaths, strange spaces of time, short spaces of time, crisis mode, maintenance mode. Life is short. Life is full. I never say my life is too busy. Instead, life is full. And don't you want a full life? Stop complaining; rejoice that life is full.

Your job as a novelist is, in the midst of your full life, to keep on coming back–somehow–to the novel revision process until you finish it.

Editors often say that the first chapter of a novel is superb, but the rest of the novel doesn't measure up. Writers tend to polish and polish that first chapter, but get distracted by a full life and don't polish the rest. Don't let that happen to your story.

Stay the course.

Walk the Talk

When life interferes with the writing of your story, come back and reread this chapter. And work.

28

Please Yourself First

One of the few things I know about writing is this: spend it all, shoot it, play it, lose it, all, right away, every time. Do not hoard what seems good for a better place in the book, or for another book; give it, give it all, give it now.

—Annie Dillard, naturalist and essayist

Uh-oh. You got those critiques and your readers didn't think your story was perfect.

I hear the groans and sighs. I see how tired you are and that you thought you were finished, but maybe–that little voice won't let go of the idea–you need to do one more big change in plot.

Yes. It happens. You may feel that the major revision you just finished is a failure.

No. You mustn't think of it that way! The revision you just finished is a major step on the way to a novel that will proudly display your name as author!

How do you face another revision right after you've just done a revision? With courage and determination, just as you faced this revision. Most novels will go through three or four major revisions, and some need much more than that. The key is to hold a standard in your mind and not be satisfied until you reach that.

Walk the Talk

What is your standard? Did this draft please you?

Think honestly about what your next step should be. Submission or revision?

29

The Best Job I Know to Do

I can't understand why a person will take a year to write a novel when he can easily buy one for a few dollars.
—Fred Allen, humorist

Does the revision process ever end?

Yes!

How do you know when your novel is ready to send off to a publisher?

You don't. This is all I know: I can't think of anything else to do that will make it better. None of my critiquers are sparking anything that raises niggling questions. I've done the best job I know how to do at this time. Unless I get feedback from someone that takes me in new directions, there's nothing more I know to do.

Then I send it off, unapologetically. Even if it gets rejections from everyone, I stand by what I said: I've done the best job I know to do at this time of my life.

Walk the Talk

To your friends, readers, fans, and family, repeat these words: Right now, this is the best story that I know how to tell. Send the story out into the world.

30

Live. Read. Write.

Many people believe that stories are told to put people to sleep. I tell mine to wake them up.
—*Nachman of Bratslav, rabbi*

What do you do after you turn in your manuscript?

Allow yourself to be empty, and expect nothing else. Follow your whims and read. Allowing poetry to fill the empty spots. Live.

Read. Sometimes, in the heat of revision, I don't read other novels. But then, like a starving person, I gorge on novels. I take in words and story, so I can give out again.

I go back to another novel that's sitting forlorn in my drawer, one that I didn't know how to revise, but I knew wasn't ready to go out, either. I re-read it, play around with sentences, phrases, here and there. Have I lived long enough to be ready to tackle this one again?

Or, I play with voices and language and ideas. Is this the start of a new story?

And every time I check my email, hope makes my heart skip a beat. . . .

Walk the Talk

Pick out a new author and read three of his or her stories. Tape record an old story and listen to it as you exercise. Use odd writing prompts to play around with language. Write essays, letters, blog posts, those things that fall by the wayside in the heat of finishing a novel. In short, live.

But mostly, trust that writing is a cyclical process. You will write again. You will revise again. Right now? Just live that full life. Wait for a new beginning, for a project that will grab your heart and demand to be written.

DARCY PATTISON

Growing up, author Darcy Pattison (**www.darcypattison.com**) wanted to be an astronaut. Instead, she writes about aliens in her early chapter book series, *ALIEN, INC. SERIES (Mims House)*, which includes *Kell, the Alien; Kell and the Horse Apple Parade; Kell and the Giants;* and *Kell and the Detectives*. Published in eight languages, her middle grade novels include: *Saucy and Bubba: A Hansel and Gretel Tale (Mims House); The Girl, the Gypsy and the Gargoyle (Mims House);* and *Vagabond (Mims House)*. Recent nature books for children include: *Abayomi, the Brazilian Puma: The True Story of an Orphaned Cub*

(Mims House); *Wisdom, the Midway Albatross* (Mims House), a Starred Review in Publisher's Weekly; *Desert Baths* (Arbordale), an NSTA Outstanding Science Trade Book 2013; and, *Prairie Storms* (Arbordale).

Other eBooks for writers include *Start Your Novel*; *How to Write a Children's Picture Book*; and *The Book Trailer Manual*. Recent teacher resource books include *Common Core ELA Activities: Month by Month Writing, Speaking and Listening Activities Aligned with the Common Core (2012); What is Common Core? (2013);* and *Writing for the Common Core (2014).* Darcy Pattison is the 2007 recipient of Arkansas Governor's Arts Awards for her work in Children's Literature.

For more see **darcypattison.com/about**

Sign up for news about more how-to-write books at **MimsHouse.com/newsletter.**

For online video courses with Darcy Pattison, see **Mimshouse.com/courses**

Manufactured by Amazon.ca
Bolton, ON

27277837R00068